# A Manual for Teacher Training in the African American Church

# Dr. Oneal Sandidge

CHICAGO SPECTRUM PRESS
EVANSTON, IL

Copyright © 1996 by Oneal Sandidge

CHICAGO SPECTRUM PRESS
1571 SHERMAN AVE., ANNEX C
EVANSTON, IL 60201
800-594-5190

All rights reserved. Except for appropriate use in critical reviews or works of scholarship, the reproduction or use of this work in any form or by any electronic, mechanical, or other means now known or hereafter invented, including photocopying and recording, and in any information storage and retrieval system, is forbidden without written permission of the authors or publisher.

Printed in the U.S.A.
10 9 8 7 6 5 4 3 2 1

ISBN: 1-886094-31-4
Library of Congress Catalog Number: 95-083799

# DEDICATION

This book is dedicated to God, my parents, the late Wardie Sandidge and Hattie Dawson Sandidge of Monroe, Virginia; my wife, Janice Oliver; my children, Ieke Monique and Jermaine Oneal Sandidge; my godson, Ronnie A. Clark; my godparents, Mr. and Mrs. James Carter; and Mr. Derrick Adkin.

*Rodney Guy Oliver*

# Special Recognitions

There are many people to recognize for this work. They include:

God Almighty for strength to write; Rev. Ronnie Clark, typist and research assistant.

*Readers* who read chapters or the entire manuscript and/or gave comments: Dr. James L. Campbell, Chairman of English Department, Lynchburg College; Dr. Marion Poindexter, Professor of Christian Education, Drew University; Dr. Donald Griggs of Livermore, California; Dr. Jonathan Jackson, Professor of Christian Education, Interdenominational Theological Seminary (I.T.C.); and Dr. Charles Foster, Professor, Candler School of Theology at Emory University.

*Travel assistance:* Mrs. Sally Dawson; Mr. Sidney Miller; and Mrs. Arlean S. Hunter.

*Special Thanks* to a world-class runner and friend who took time to give me advice and encouragement for this project; Mr. Derrick Adkins.

Special Recognitions to churches: New Second Buffalo Baptist Church, Nathalie, VA; Greater Peaceful Zion Baptist Church, Lynchburg, VA; and White Rock Baptist Church, Arrington, VA.

# CREDITS

Special permissions to use works include:

Religious Education Press, Birmingham, Alabama: *Improving Church Education, Renewing the Sunday School and the CCD, How to Evaluate a C.E. Program, Religious Education and Theology, Infusion of American Content in the School Curriculum,* and *Urban Church Education.*

Black Light Fellowship: *Black Presence in the Bible.*

Discipleship Resources: *Christian Education — Journey of Black Americans* (copyright 1985), and *Educational Ministries with Blacks* (copyright 1974).

Standard Publishing: *Superintend With Success* by Guy Leavitt.

Griggs Educational Services: *Teaching Teachers to Teach.*

Rev. Joseph Moore: Artwork.

Professor Alexis Joyner: Artwork.

Rev. Ronnie Clark: Poetry.

Mr. Rodney Oliver: Artwork.

Mr. Michael Anthony Johnson: Artwork.

Mr. Fred Crews: Poetry.

Mr. Antonio Dawson: Poetry.

# TABLE OF CONTENTS

Dedication ..................................................................................................... 3
Special Recognitions ..................................................................................... 4
Credits ........................................................................................................... 5
Foreword ....................................................................................................... 7
Introduction .................................................................................................. 9
Poetry ........................................................................................................... 13

**CHAPTER 1**
Roles of the Teacher ................................................................................... 17
**CHAPTER 2**
Evaluating Sunday School Literature in the African American Church ...... 25
**CHAPTER 3**
The Purposes of Sunday School Literature ................................................ 26
**CHAPTER 4**
Components for the Lesson Plan ............................................................... 44
**CHAPTER 5**
Media Tools ................................................................................................ 53
**CHAPTER 6**
Suggested Workshops for the African American Church ........................... 55
**CHAPTER 7**
Future Suggestions for Christian Education in the African American
Church ........................................................................................................ 57

# Foreword

Dr. Oneal Sandidge's Manual for Teacher Training has presented · most urgently needed resource for the African American Church. In a · time when the responsibility for the moral and cultural education of African Americans rest squarely on the shoulders of the African American Church, this important work calls us to reaffirm the richness of our proud heritage. In very clear terms this work demonstrates the cultural and biblical soundness of developing an African American Hermeneutic which addresses the social and spiritual needs of the African American Church and community. I applaud Dr. Sandidge for having the courage to insist that Sunday School Teachers give as much attention to the preparation of their lesson plans as would a master teacher in the public and private school systems. Equally courageous is the call for scrutiny in the process of selecting teachers for the Sunday School. For too long the church has allowed Sunday School Teachers to present unplanned class presentations. This is true in part because of the absence of a thorough oversight committee assigned to take seriously the importance of the Sunday School to the overall Christian Education Ministry of the church.

Every person involved in the Christian Education Ministry of the church will be greatly aided by the attention Dr. Sandidge gives to the critical role of evaluating the teacher and the literature used in the Sunday School Department. This book lifts the standards by which Sunday Schools are to be evaluated. It also sets guidelines which can be easily implemented.

Special thanks are extended to Dr. Sandidge for his leadership in the First Annual Christian Education Leadership Institute sponsored by the Hampton University Ministers' Conference.

—Dr. Michael A. Battle Sr.
University Chaplain, Hampton University

*Professor Alexis Joyner*

# Introduction

*And God has appointed in the church first apostles, second prophets, third teachers; then deeds of power, then gifts of healing, forms of assistance, forms of leadership, various kinds of tongues. Are all apostles? Are all prophets? Are all teachers?... But strive for the greater gifts. And I will show you a still more excellent way (1st Corinthians 12:28-31).*

Many Sunday schools are looking for ways to improve teaching in the church schools. Many Sunday schools dispense training for their superintendents, teachers, and teacher-aides. Some have teacher training once a month; while others have training once a year or not at all. Some churches are losing a portion of their members due to inadequate, untrained teachers. In any case, teacher training is very portentous for the church Sunday school. Teachers should be carefully selected. An educator who teaches in public school is a good applicant for teaching in the Sunday school, but not every public school teacher is a Christian. In any case, Christian education training is needed for all teachers in Christian education. Some pastors know the need for a solid educational program, including the need for trained teachers. Other pastors hinder the Christian educational program because of their limited educational background. One should not impede nor contest education because of one's educational background. For example, limitation of educational training, whether one did not see the need for education or could not receive an education for other reasons, does not prohibit endorsement of a sound Christian educational program. There is definite need for more teacher training in the African American Church and mixed settings. The role of the teacher is very important in the African American Church.

The teacher can "make" or "break" the church. Poor teaching methods may drive students from the Sunday school or from the church. To be a good teacher, one should seek training and constantly update teach-

# Introduction

ing skills. Training should include learning how to select the appropriate literature for students. This manual is designed for teaching graduate students or seminarians, teachers themselves, and perhaps all who might be accountable for teacher training in the African American Church, whether as volunteer, nonprofessional, or professional church educator. The "knowing" of how to teach is always an ongoing process. According to author and religious educator, Donald Griggs, "The teacher is more an artist than he/she is a scientist" (1). The teacher should paint a picture to encourage the student to attend Sunday school, Bible-study, and, of course, the African American Church regular worship service. To prepare this picture, the teacher should study a lesson long enough to relate to life experiences. This means carefully selecting Sunday school literature. The person in charge of selecting Sunday school literature for the African American Church should be cautious during the selection process.

There are many companies which market Sunday school literature. Some companies have literature appropriate for the church; however, many companies have unclear artwork or spurious images with the literature. Many companies produce good artwork but provide poor content or vice-versa. Presently there is no known company that publishes Sunday school literature solely from the Afrocentric perspective. For example, there is no known Sunday school literature that presents God at work in the African Biblical heritage. Afrocentric literature is needed for the African American student. As I discussed with pastors who want a totally Afrocentric curriculum, those pastors have forgotten that one should be "spoon-fed," not chocked with food. In other words, bits and pieces of Afrocentric ideas should be integrated in the curriculum. It would be a cultural shock to make a change overnight. However, if an Afrocentric image is not seen, studied, and taught in our churches, the student may have a blurred vision of African roots. Many African American Churches and racially mixed settings should consider modifying their present curriculum to include the teaching of the African heritage.

In this manual, it is suggested that the African American Church student is often "turned off" because of poor teacher presentations. Many teachers do not understand how to write lesson plans and are unsure about the best content for students. Chapter One will deliberate the role of the teacher; Chapter Two will examine evaluating the teacher; Chapter Three will consider evaluating Sunday school literature; Chapter Four will review developing lesson plans; Chapter Five will discuss using media resources; Chapter Six will suggest workshops for teachers in the African American Church; and Chapter Seven will provide suggestions for future Christian education in the African American Church.

The terms: Negro, Black, and African American will be used interchangeably, referring to the same people. The latter term is a more modern term reflecting the African heritage and American culture.

*Michael Anthony Johnson*

# Poetry

The Sunday school teacher must continue to use creative methods. Poetry is just one way to be creative. The following poems express birth, growth, living, and survival.

# The Two Births

Fred R. Crews

In this world there are two births.
One we've all been through which I'll tell you about first.
It's the birth when two chefs come together
with their bowls, their spoons, or their stirrers.
They took their large bowl and poured in ingredients to start,
like a tablespoon of KNOWLEDGE and a big chunk of HEART.
This is a good beginning but they are not done,
so they added a whole heaping of LOVE and a gift from the one above
The gift from GOD is the most important to thee,
for it gives life to the child to be born.
This should bring forth the first birth,
But, let's evaluate the second, for what it's worth.
Unlike the first, the second is not guaranteed,
only a few are given this deed.
The ones who realize the key to being born again,
is to give back their soul and walk with their life-long friend.
The Savior is the One who will always be there
to guide and strengthen and show that He cares.
So wake up my children and realize today,
that life after life begins by following the ALMIGHTY'S WAY.

# THE ORIGIN OF LIFE

RONNIE A. CLARK

Life is always in question.
Trees have an origin.
Animals have an origin.
People have an origin.
All things have origin.
Have you ever thought
about the origin of life?
It started years ago,
before our time.
A child has an origin
a parent is somewhere
a mother bears the pain
a father feels the trembles.
Who creates the soul?
The heart of humanity that
links to make us one.
Who creates the
origin of life?
Who makes the constellations
and its infiniteness?
Who makes day and night?
Who creates students?
Who creates life?
Who creates the Sunday school?
God does.
Who did God work through?
The answer lies in the origin of life.

# Why Can't I Have

Antonio Marcellus Dawson

Why can't I have:
dreams and hopes of happy
children not on dope.
Why can't I have:
a place to call my own
that's free and alone.
Why can't I have:
a voice that talks
on the same level as you.
Why can't I have:
the right to live
love and dance.
Why can't I have:
no dimensions, yet;
claim my inventions.
Why can't I have:
a piece of the pie
just before I die.

# Roles of the Teacher

*The gifts he gave were that some would be apostles, some prophets, some pastors and teachers, to equip the saints for the work of the ministry, for building up the body of Christ, until all of us come to the unity of the Faith and of the knowledge of the Son of God, to maturity, to the measure of the Full stature of Christ (Ephesians 4:11-13).*

The role of the Sunday school teacher is to teach the Word of God in a way African Americans can comprehend as God's Divine Word. The teacher should always remember that Holy Scripture is the authentic Sunday school book. The Holy Spirit provides insights for the teacher. The teacher should be spirit-filled, and willing to allow the spirit to provide directions in the course of teaching.

More specifically, the roles of the teacher are: 1. To provide rehumanization, 2. To know what he or she might be teaching, 3. To spend time planning, and 4. To choose the right teaching method.

Whether the church has a mixed congregation or otherwise, if the church is labeled African American, then teaching from that perspective should prevail. The African American Church should teach from the African American heritage. Teaching from the African American heritage is teaching from the Afrocentric and American experiences. Molefi Kete Asante states in *The Afrocentric Idea:*

> Afrocentricity is the most complete philosophical totalization of the African being-at-the-center of his or her existence. It is not merely an artistic or literary movement. Not only is it an individual or collective quest for authenticity, but it is above all, the total use of method to effect psychological, political, social, cultural, and economic change. The Afrocentric idea is beyond the colonizing the mind. (125)

# Roles of the Teacher

There is a special need for teachers to reflect the African heritage experience in the African American Church School. Dr. Keith Allan Chism states in his dissertation:

> The term that best identifies the Black Sunday School with the historical plight of African Americans is survival. The African American Sunday School has made the gospel relevant to the struggles of an oppressed people. (112)

The teacher should include lessons that help students deal with everyday problems. This means that the teacher should consider the entire makeup of each student. Given such consideration, the teacher might recall the words of Edward Franklin Frazier about the African American:

> In studying any phase of the character and the development of the social and cultural life of the Negro in the United States, one must recognize from the beginning that because of the manner in which Negroes were captured in Africa and enslaved, they were practically stripped of their social heritage. ( 9)

The social context of African Americans has been weakened due to the mistreatment of African Americans, but was never totally destroyed. This means that the teacher has a greater task to teach African heritage to recapture any social heritage that may have been lost. Teaching should include the sociological makeup of African Americans not only for what has been lost, but to rekindle one's present state.

## First role of the teacher — Rehumanization

The first role of teacher is what Williard A. Williams in *Educational Ministries for Blacks* calls **rehumanization**. Rehumanization is exposing the student to new values. The term comes from the "twoness" concept of W.E.B. Dubois. According to Williard Williams, W.E. B. Dubois explains:

> One ever feels twoness, an American, a Negro: two souls, two thoughts, two unreconciled strivings, two warring ideals in one dark body, whose dogged strength alone keeps it from being torn asunder. (16)

Each day a person might experience racism. Williard A. Williams calls today's concept of twoness, rehumanization, which includes racism as a dehumanizing and destructive social force. Teaching/learning should inculcate positive concepts. Many of these African heritage values are lost in the mind of the African American student. Williard Williams lists five steps for retooling rehumanization:

> 1. The development of personhood, 2. The self-determination of persons in society, 3. The development of skills, habits, and values necessary for controlling destiny, 4. Gaining appreciation and pride in one's heritage, and 5. The appropriation of the Christian faith. (17)

### Development of Personhood

The teacher should be aware of ways to rehumanize the African American student. The development of personhood is important for students. The teacher should understand that the student is a human being. Many students are depressed because of their unstable home situations. The teaching experience is another chance to make the student gain confidence about self. The teacher can help students develop personhood by teaching students how to handle and affirm cultural differences, and to recognize and affirm the history and culture of minorities.

### The Self-Determination of Persons in Society

The teacher might teach students to understand the self-determination of people in society. Self-determination of people in society is an empowering element. When the student fails, self-determination allows the student to make decisions that might lead to recovering success. Self-determination allows the student to participate within structures that influence and govern life-styles. The wholeness of people are learned in the self-determination process. It is important for the student to be cognitive of what is going on in society. Society goes beyond the area in which a person lives. Students may visit other cities, or other African American businesses and residential areas. It is crucial to expose students to new values. The self-determination process awakens the student so that he or she is inspired to overcome suppressive or repressive external forces through their mental psyche development. Teaching students about the self-determination of people is teaching students to understand community and to develop vibrant, healthy relationships with others.

### The Development of Skills, Habits, and Values for Controlling Destiny

In developing skills, habits, and values, the teacher should state the problem which exists. For example, if the problem is lack of job training, the teacher should provide methods to encourage the student to seek a new job. Providing hope is the key. Some students are "spiritless" because of socioeconomic conditions. Many students have lost hope because of the lack of African traditions in our society. One cannot dwell on past failures and fully succeed in the future.

### Gaining Appreciation and Pride in One's Heritage

Students are rehumanized when they gain appreciation and pride in their heritage. Students should be taught to make decisions for themselves. The teacher can teach students to appreciate and have pride in their heritage. The teacher may teach students to be familiar with positive African American role models.

### The Appropriation of the Christian Faith

The appropriation of Christian faith is of much value. Every student should have the right to view God and Christ from his or her own experience. In other words, the African American student should be able to decide on the appearance of Jesus, see his blue eyes in illustrations, and at the same time see the Black Jesus for identity purposes. It is wise to view religion in relation to one's social and physical environment. Students need to know that Jesus Christ died for everyone. Faith is not only believing but living a Christian life. Faith lives and is at work in the hearts of Christians. Jesus must be seen in all walks of life. He ate with sinners, and knew of poverty. Rehumanization may be developed if the teacher instructs students about the African background, and stresses the makeup of the African American family. Instruction should be from the African heritage perspective and about the African American family.

## Second Role of the Teacher — Know what Should Be Taught

The second role of the teacher in what Bennie Goodwin, in *Steps to Dynamic Teaching*, calls *The Law of the Teacher*. "The teacher must know that which she or he would teach" (3). Bennie Goodwin states that the teacher should also study the lesson. The teacher should also plan the lesson, gather the materials, choose the method, and plan the procedure.

Preparing lesson plans involve many hours of review. A good review takes place when the teacher knows his or her teaching assignment. Effective teachers do not wait until the last minute to prepare lessons. It is not wise for a teacher to wait until the night before or the day of the class for lesson preparation. One needs to prepare for teaching by praying for spiritual insights and gathering material and content information far in advance of class. The Bible or the Word of God is always first and is dominate over any commentary, dictionary, or any other source, including teacher and student manuals.

## THIRD ROLE OF THE TEACHER — PLANNING

In planning the lesson, two basics should be considered: 1. The age group, goals, and objectives for students, and 2. Gathering materials for teaching.

Planning is very important. The age of the students one will be teaching should be kept in mind. The age group will help determine how one will write the goals and objectives for the lesson. If one does not know the goals and objectives of the lesson, one is teaching in what I call the "darkness of teaching."

The gathering of materials means reading any available source(s) of material(s), and looking at more than one version of the Bible. The *New Revised Standard Version of the Bible* is recommended as one biblical source because teachers realize the need for teaching "standard" English, as well as accepting dialect or *Black English*. I am not suggesting doing away with other versions of the Bible, but the emphasis should be on a version of the Bible that students can clearly understand. After one knows the age group and has decided on the objectives and goals and gathered the materials, choosing the right teaching method is next.

## FOURTH ROLE OF THE TEACHER — CHOOSING THE RIGHT TEACHING METHOD

Choosing the right teaching method is very important. Will one ask questions, use projects, story-telling, audiovisuals, or lecture (the art of asking questions is discussed in the chapter on evaluating Sunday school literature)?

When one knows the method, it will be easier to plan the lesson procedure. To plan the lesson procedure, the teacher will simply have the format before him or her and will know what comes first, second, and thereafter (Goodwin, *Steps,* 3-4). Once the lesson has been planned and studied, the teacher can then teach the lesson effectively.

Roles of the Teacher

*Rev. Joseph A. Moore*

# Chapter 2

# Evaluating the Teacher in the African American Church

Teachers should be evaluated at least twice during the year. The Christian Education Board, or the Minister/Director of Christian Education should evaluate the teacher. In the event that a church does not have a Board or Minister of Christian Education, then the superintendent or person in charge of Christian education could evaluate the teacher. The superintendent reports to the Christian Education Board or the Director of Christian Education for direction. The Christian Education Board and/or the Christian Education Director reports to the pastor or the selected person or board for instructions. If there is no Christian Education Board or Christian Education Director, the superintendent or person in charge reports to the pastor for leadership instruction. The following might be considered for evaluating teachers in the box on page 24.

For teens or adults, students could complete evaluation forms for leaders' review. For example, the Christian Education Director or its board (or superintendent, if none exists) may use similar questions with a blank beside each for students to evaluate the teacher on a 1 – 10 scale to show the effectiveness of the teacher. One on the scale indicates a low or poor performance, five indicates average performance, and ten indicates a high or excellent teacher performance. One may find the average of each evaluation sheet, then find the average of all sheets to derive a final evaluation. Only leaders should have access to evaluation files. At no point should an evaluator state his or her name.

# Evaluating the Teacher

The evaluations along with observation reports are important to leaders. A good Christian Education Board or Christian Education Director and its superintendent will visit the classroom once or twice a year.

### QUESTIONS FOR EVALUATING TEACHERS

1. Is the teacher on time?
2. Is the teacher prepared for the job?
3. Does the teacher communicate effectively with the age group?
4. Do students seem to enjoy attending the class?
5. Is the teacher creative (goes beyond using the regular literature)?
6. Does the teacher continually demonstrate a "saved" life?
7. Is there good rapport with the teacher/pastor-leader/minister of Christian education?
8. Is there a continuation of good attitude (teacher shows the desire to teach)?
9. Does the teacher present lessons according to the lesson design?
10. Does the teacher place strong emphasis upon African American traditions?

# Chapter 3

# Evaluating Sunday School Literature in the African American Church

The purpose of this chapter is to provide guidelines for evaluating Sunday school literature specifically for the African American Church. This chapter highlights reasons for evaluating Sunday school literature and provides directions for improvement, and how evaluation provides information to the learner and educator about the teaching/learning experience. Prior to evaluating Sunday school literature, the content sought is quite important. Curriculum for the African American Church might include biblical content and examples from the Afrocentric experiences. For example, one could read *The Black Presence in the Bible* by Rev. Walter Arthur McCray and find a lot of teaching content for developing an African American Curriculum. In addition, one might look at some of Dr. Cain Felder's books, such as *Troubling Biblical Waters, Stony the Road We Trod*, or *The Original African Heritage Study Bible*. One may acquire information from many Afrocentric books to develop a Sunday school curriculum for African Americans. Another book to help teachers glance at general curricula is *Infusion of African and African American Content in the School Curriculum: Proceedings of the First National Conference, October, 1989* presents a curriculum for African Americans. Regrettably, this report does not go into details for religious education, but rather discusses private or public education. The model can be helpful in creating a curriculum for the African American Church school. The authors deliberate the Afrocentric goal of education: competence, confidence, and consciousness of Afro-Americans educational needs (13). The person selecting Sunday school literature for the church curriculum should pos-

# Evaluating the Sunday School Literature

sess all three: competence, confidence, and consciousness. If one is going to teach in the church, knowing the literature evaluation process is very important. Sunday school literature needs to be evaluated by denominational leaders and Christian Education Directors, prior to endorsement for church/denominational use.

An important part of a Sunday school teacher's task is to make sure that the literature is appropriate for the age level being taught. If the literature is too difficult for students, the teacher should report such discrepancies to those persons who adopted the literature. According to Dr. Bennie Goodwin, a successful leader gets things done. This goes beyond "acting and reacting, achieving, and accomplishing," but "one must get the right things done" (*The Effective Leader* 11-12). When teaching Sunday school, the teacher must make sure that students have text(s) that they can comprehend.

## THE PURPOSES OF SUNDAY SCHOOL LITERATURE

What are the purposes of Sunday school literature? Sunday school literature: 1. Affirms the faith of the community, and in the case of the African American Church, affirms the faith of the African American Community, 2. Demonstrates to the student a sense of belonging, 3. Provides positive images, and 4. Teaches the Word of God.

### AFFIRMING THE FAITH OF THE COMMUNITY

According to a *Brethren Press Curriculum Guide,* by affirming the faith of the community, Sunday school students see how persons of all ages are drawn into the faith community. Students might be able to encourage friends and relatives who are not part of the faith community to join based on their knowledge of the faith community (11).

### THE SENSE OF BELONGING

The literature ought to provide a sense of belonging. If one is unable to feel involved in lessons, one will not own the lesson. African Americans need to understand the biblical stories which discuss the African American heritage. Many times, African Americans only hear stories from the white perspective. African American heritage is not the only heritage to be studied, but African American heritage should be known. Rev. Walter McCray states:

We believe that this present treatment of the Black presence in the Bible offers a fresh perspective for a growing constituency of Christian Black educators and learners who seek to maintain a good respect for reliable Biblical and historical information. In style, we have sought to take scholarly material and make it intellectually digestible to the common reader. Those who are teachers should discover quickly how easily they can grasp and share this message with their learners (xi).

It is important to read and discern this fresh perspective to feel the sense of belonging. In other words, to belong is to be a part of something when one combines: reading, studying, and digesting. Also, African Americans should never allow past negative comments to interfere with new modes of thinking. Mary A. Love states in *Renewing the Sunday School and the CCD*: "If one only hears the negative and knows that she or he is Black, it is fair to assume that one will begin to develop a negative self-image" (163).

## Providing Positive Images

The African American student needs to see positive images in the Sunday school literature. Many publishers are simply concerned about the majority market, that group which buys the most texts. In most cases, the publisher will find that its majority market will be non-African American, unless the company is producing materials solely for African Americans. Joint Educational Developers (JED) indirectly made a joint effort to insert Blackness in curriculum. JED suggests that curriculum for African Americans do the following:

> Affirm Blackness as a gift of God, continue the quest for a positive self-identity, sustain a desire to participate in the continuing struggle for Black liberation, justice and human fulfillment, develop critical thinking abilities and decision-making skills, promote attitudes of respect for self and others in the community of faith, establish cultural bridges of understanding and harmonious relationships among peoples of different cultures, religions, and ethnic orientation, foster cooperative search for solutions to critical issues, promote understanding for the need to preserve and maintain cultural and artistic expressions in worship and the arts, affirm the goal of social reform through democratic processes and applications of Christian principles, proclaim the liberation of all persons in the name of Christ, respond creatively to daily challenges and assaults on one's humanity, help learners utilize biblical insights in trying to orga-

nize, plan and implement programs and activities that humanize and aid in the realization of God given potentials; thereby consciously and purposefully seeking to transform the world to be what God intended, aid in understanding the roots of racism and how it affects all Christians, inform learners about the nature of social, economic, and political injustices perpetuated by society on ethnic Americans, strengthen knowledge of the African, African American, and Caribbean experience, assist in identifying and eradicating stereotypes of multi-ethnic Christians, identify black models of achievement and accomplishment in American, African and Caribbean societies, illuminate and explore the totality of the Black Religious Experience, place in proper perspective the significant role of Black Americans as participants and contributors in the growth and development of the American nation, and enhance the study of American diversity and celebrate multi-culturalism. (*Joint Educational Development Manual — Perspectives in Church Education*)

### Teaching the Word of God

The most important purpose for Sunday School literature is teaching the Word of God. More and more teachers are neglecting careful review of the Word of God in Sunday school literature. The Word of God must be correctly stated from a given Bible version and a true theological meaning should be seen in the lesson content. The Word of God convicts one of sin (Jeremiah 23:29). The Word points one to Christ (John 1:36), and the Word is instrumental for learners to become saved (John 1:12; Peter 1:13). Jesus commanded Christians to teach (Matthew 28:19-20).

The evaluation of Sunday school literature is very important for Christians; and African American Christians must never forget that they are as important as any people in this world. As African Americans recall their own roots, many will press toward the mark of creating a curriculum for African American students.

## Reasons for Evaluating Sunday School Literature

Are there reasons for evaluating Sunday school literature? Yes, there are many reasons for evaluating Sunday school literature: 1. Evaluating Sunday school literature establishes the areas and directions for growth, and 2. Evaluation also provides information to the learner and educator about his or her progress in the teaching/learning experience.

According to Dewitte Campbell Wyckoff in *How to Evaluate Your C.E. Program,* "Evaluation is a process of comparing what is with what ought to be, in order to determine areas and directions for improvement" (9). Evaluation informs the teacher of the students' interests; and, after evaluating, the one who selects Sunday school literature can then form a basis for the selection of the Sunday school literature.

## Evaluating Sunday School Literature Establishes the Areas and Directions for Growth

If the Sunday school literature is evaluated and it is found the student is not learning at the teacher's desired pace, the teacher should consider modifying his or her plans to meet the needs of the student. In other words, when the teacher rethinks or rewrites lesson plans, considering the need of the student is important. Generally speaking, one could evaluate Sunday school literature by looking at selected curricula units. A unit includes all the lessons designed for a given period of time. Any unit may be selected for evaluation because most units use the same form. The structure should include a topic, introduction, and scripture for all units.

## Evaluating Also Provides Information to the Learner and Educator about his or her Progress in the Teaching/Learning Experience

The evaluation of Sunday school literature is very portentous to both students and Christian educators because evaluation provides valuable information to the learner and educator about his or her progress in the teaching/learning experience. An evaluation of Sunday school literature should include reviewing the theology in literature. Theology could stand in the background of religious educational theory, taking over the content, and sometimes providing a false evaluation to the learner (Miller, Randolph 40). A false evaluation hinders the learning process. It is important to be careful about the theologies embedded in Sunday school literature. If one considers theology of vital importance, then goals and objectives can be easily planned.

The student and teacher will quickly realize if the goal of the lesson was achieved. If the lesson was not learned, one knows that the methods used were not effective in accomplishing the goal. The goal could be beyond the capabilities of the learners, or maybe the students and teacher did not understand the goal (Cully 71).

### Goals and Objectives are Bases for Evaluating Sunday School Literature

Goals and objectives are the foundations on which lessons are written; therefore, it is very important to evaluate goals and objectives. Donald Griggs states the following about goals and objectives:

> Goals are big enough to spend a whole lifetime pursuing...are beyond our reach; We will never fully achieve the goals of Christian living. Goals give us directions for our teaching, learning, relating, deciding, etc. Goals are too general to use for planning and evaluating teaching activities. Objectives are specific. Objectives are written in terms of what students can be expected to accomplish, in particular through learning activities. Objectives are achievable. Objectives are very helpful guidelines for teachers to use in planning and evaluating teaching activities. (13)

Educators should carefully look at the goals and objectives of each unit and each lesson. When evaluating goals and objectives, make sure that goals are not confused with objectives. Goals are general; objectives are specific (goals and objectives will be discussed in Chapter Four). Even if the goal is adequate, certain goals might not be met until students are more mature. In any event, teachers should reevaluate and restructure the learning process each year as necessary (Cully 71). For example, perhaps the previous year the conversion experience was taught, and if asked, some teenagers will be able to describe and write about their conversion experience, while others will accept various descriptions of conversion experiences. Goals and objectives should help educators realize what students can accomplish. It is then crucial for leaders to evaluate Sunday school literature to make sure that lessons meet the criteria for the established goals and objectives. In evaluating Sunday school literature, one might establish some guidelines for evaluating. The following guidelines are recommended.

> **GUIDELINES FOR EVALUATING SUNDAY SCHOOL LITERATURE**
> *(Developed from Dr. Marion Poindexter's 1986 Class Curriculum, Drew University)*
>
> **CRITERION 1**
> Is Sunday school literature Christian in aim and content?
>
> **CRITERION 2**
> Is Sunday school literature directed to the needs of growing persons?
>
> **CRITERION 3**
> Does Sunday school literature take into account how a Christian undergoes Christian growth?
>
> **CRITERION 4**
> Does Sunday school literature help Sunday school leaders relate to the total experience of students?
>
> **CRITERION 5**
> Does the literature provide ancestry identification for students?
>
> **CRITERION 6**
> Does the artwork provide enrichment for African American students?
>
> **CRITERION 7**
> Does the activity packet provide a learning experience?

**CRITERION 1: IS SUNDAY SCHOOL LITERATURE CHRISTIAN IN AIM AND CONTENT?**

What about Scripture? Scripture is very important when it comes to selecting Sunday school literature. Does it cultivate a response to the Gospel? Sunday school literature should be related to the Bible in that the Bible provides the total Christian heritage. Thus, the Scripture could give insight into change. How we can depend upon God while experiencing change?

Scripture may be connected to African American experiences through "Story;" whereby, one can feel the power of God in people's lives (Crockett 2). African Americans should be taught that there are many ways to learn Scripture. The classroom teacher should attempt to reach all levels of students.

# Evaluating the Sunday School Literature

Ronald C. Doll suggests that one should weigh theological considerations. In other words, one must know if the Sunday school literature is written for Christians, or it is written to invite nonbelievers to consider becoming a Christian. For example, some Christians would want to ask:

Are the materials based on the Scriptures as the major instructional source for Christian education? Do they provide a faithful record of, and a friendly commentary on, biblical events and teachings, rather than an interpretation of events and teachings that is actually or potentially negative? Do the materials speak with assurance of God's power and goodness in performing miracles, including the great miracles of the Resurrection and the Virgin Birth? Do they uphold the Bible's validity in helping people solve problems today? Do they emphasize the stable, dependable values that the Scriptures teach? Do the materials encourage the learner to commit himself to Jesus Christ as his personal Savior? Do they make it clear that the learner's right relationship with God is a necessary precondition to his having right relationships with his fellow men? Do they help those learners who have given themselves to Christ to increase their faith and trust in him? (7)

Evaluators should then ask: Do the materials state understandable and acceptable objectives? Do they contain specific data, main ideas, and key concepts in balanced proportion and arrangement? Do they achieve a focus on main ideas and key concepts to which all other content clearly contributes? (7-8)

To help determine worth, teachers might ask: Are the materials appropriate to learners' abilities, needs, and interests? Do they cause learners to repeat important experiences and review important ideas? Do the materials increase in difficulty throughout the span of years they cover? (8)

One might look at learning by asking: Do the materials provide a variety of ways to stimulate learning? Do they contain and suggest supplementary aids to learning? Do they make thrifty use of the time available for learning? (8)

Also, one can look at hints for teaching. Evaluators may ask: Are inexperienced teachers able to use the materials without difficulty or confusion? Are teachers' guides or teachers' editions of the materials genuinely helpful, suggesting procedures that make teaching easier and more effective? Do they contain suggestions for teacher planning and growth and for ways of evaluating teaching and learning? (8)

According to a guide reproduced by Brethren Press, one should consider the following questions about the biblical and theological roots:

1. What references are there to the activity of God...in history? In Jesus? As recorded in Scripture?

2. In what ways is the good news of God's action evident...through Scripture? Through the person and work of Jesus Christ?

3. What activities are suggested that develop/deepen faith perspectives?

4. How are persons helped to reflect biblically/theologically on their experience?

5. What suggestions are made for learning how to act on their theological reflections? (*Brethren Press Curriculum Guide* 11)

These questions about the Bible and theology should lead one to think about the faith community. One should question whether or not the literature is Christian in aim and in content. Does the literature cultivate a response to the gospel? The literature should have some relevance to the Bible and to the gospel. The literature should consider the total Christian heritage. The teacher should look at all lessons in their entirety, not just one book or unit, to see if it covers the Christian heritage, the church history, the lives of famous missionaries, martyrs, and so on. Sunday school literature should provide ways for a student to grow from childhood to adulthood. The literature should have some insight into change. In other words, the literature should offer ways for students to depend upon God while living in change.

As stated above, during the evaluation process, keep in mind the fact that whatever materials are decided upon, they should be based on the scriptures. Scripture is the major source for Christian education.

## CRITERION 2: IS SUNDAY SCHOOL LITERATURE DIRECTED TO THE NEEDS OF GROWING PERSONS?

Sunday school literature should be directed to the needs of growing persons. Growing persons are those who advance from nursery to adult stages. Growing persons do not stay at the same stage; therefore, the literature should help all levels of students. For example, senior citizens should be able to grow by learning new ways of cultivating their old ideas to refresh their minds with new insights. The literature should enhance self-value, which is needed before students consider becoming part of a group. After a student becomes a part of a group, he or she could determine what standards are needed within the group. Of course, the literature which has been taught to students will help them make such decisions.

Sunday school literature can either motivate or discourage students from attending class. A good presentation of the literature could encourage a student to be committed to Sunday school attendance. In all cases, Christian doctrines help students grow. The literature should provide essentials or basics for one's denomination. If the literature does not provide essentials, then one must decide if the literature is or is not best for that congregation/denomination. One can modify any literature, but the question which should be asked, "Do you have time or the desire to modify the literature?"

If an educator is going to use literature (as is) to relate to students, he or she should select lesson themes that will best serve his or her students. Lessons may be single-theme lessons, group graded theme lessons, or closely graded theme lessons. The single-theme lesson offers one subject for a certain number of classes and age groups. There is a general or overall theme. The same topic is taught to several age groups or departments in the Sunday school. The group graded lessons are for a certain group; such as, first, second, and third grades grouped together, or a group that includes children up to the 6th grade. Topics are geared for the entire age group. The closely graded lessons provide a different subject and a different lesson each Sunday for each grade (Leavitt 40-41). The closely graded theme lesson best meets the needs of growing persons because it supposedly relates more closely to the abilities and experiences of the students and challenges them to grow. For example, when students complete one grade, they can look forward to advancing to the next grade. Lessons should be advanced to the level of students. The disadvantage of the closely graded theme is that students are handicapped if they have to repeat a grade. In other words, students might become less motivated to learn if they are challenged on the same learning level. Sunday school literature should be directed to the needs of growing persons.

### CRITERION 3: DOES SUNDAY SCHOOL LITERATURE TAKE INTO ACCOUNT THE LAWS OF GROWTH?

All Sunday school literature should take into account the laws of growth because the laws of growth relate to Christian faith. The laws of growth deal with mental and emotional abilities of an individual. For example, too many pictures can manipulate young children's emotions when not used carefully. Young children cannot understand certain pictures. The ages of children should be considered when one looks at curriculum. Children ages four, five, or six do not desire to sit for a long period of time. A lengthy lesson plan is not appropriate for the attention span of younger children.

When evaluating curriculum, look at the concepts of the lesson. Determine the concept and whether one will use concrete or abstract ideas in the lesson. The concept is the whole picture. For example, the journey of Jesus to Jerusalem might be the concept. The concrete idea is something that one can see, hear, or do. For example, students can look at a map and see locations where Jesus traveled. An abstract idea is something that cannot be seen or touched. For example, younger students might not understand the reasons for Jesus' exploration. If abstract ideas are seen in curriculum for ages five or six, one should consider the ability levels of this age group. This age group normally cannot deal with abstract ideas. Most children are age 11 or 12 before they can realistically deal with abstract ideas.

To summarize, as people change, their needs change. Therefore, in order to provide a sound curriculum, the Sunday school literature should be selected with the laws of growth — spiritual and mental — playing an integral part of the evaluation process.

### CRITERION 4: DOES THE SUNDAY SCHOOL LITERATURE HELP LEADERS RELATE TO THE TOTAL EXPERIENCE OF STUDENTS?

Literature must possess internal educational principles; i.e., personal, analytical, and informational, as well as take into account the total life experiences of students.

Some of the internal educational principles should include comprehensiveness, balance, and sequence. Comprehensiveness is giving attention to various ages and age groups; the balance of literature is very important because balance includes material on more than one topic. There should be a balance of themes. Finally, the literature should provide sequence, or the flow of thought. The overall organization of the theme should be in sequential order. It is important to have one thought following the other. In other words, students should not become confused about the order of main points. Students should be able to follow one thought to the next thought.

### Criterion 5: Does the Literature Provide Ancestry Identification for Students?

It is timely for Sunday school literature to provide ancestry or identification for students. The African American student learns about his heritage and can identify with that heritage. The African American child should be able to visualize his or her Christian community.

When one speaks of whether Sunday school literature meets the needs of African Americans, one can consider evaluation using the following questions about the entire curriculum:

> Does the curriculum in any way perpetuate racist theologies? Does the curriculum deal realistically with racism in our pluralistic society without misrepresenting racial differences? Does the curriculum meet the needs of the Black community, both in content and skills? Is it indigenous to the Black community? For example, does it reflect the Black experience? Does it speak relevantly to the Black experience? Does the curriculum acknowledge one's social setting?

> What kind of learning theory does the curriculum presuppose? Does it show an understanding of the growth and development of the Black child, youth, and adult? Does it undergird the growth and development of the Black child, youth, and adult? Are there symbols? What words are being used to communicate concepts and ideas? Are there language barriers for the student? What symbols of cultural heritage, and economic development are found in the literature? Is there a symbol of both the Black male and female, family, church and preacher? (*Report from Krisheim II Conference on Education*)

Evaluating Sunday school questions is very important. The evaluator should consider three kinds of questions: Personal, Analytical, and Informational (Griggs 49).

## Personal Questions

Personal questions are questions that are related to the student's own life experience. The student can identify with this type of question on a personal level. Instruction guides students in their own personal decision-making and value forming thoughts (Griggs 49).

Examples of a personal level question are: "If you had been Solomon, what would you have done when...?" or "What are some times when you were asked to do something that was easy for you to do?"

## Analytical Questions

Analytical questions require students to think. There are no right answers. Questions are generally open, or have many answers and responses. One question might be asked to every student in the class. Each student could give a different response (Griggs 49).

Examples of this type of questions are: "What are some reasons why Paul would not continue persecuting Christians?" or "What do you think Paul meant when he said...?"

## Informational Questions

Lastly, informational questions require students to recall something in order to answer the question. From reading, hearing, or other ways of receiving information, students should recall some facts to answer the questions. This type of question should require right answers (Griggs 49).

Examples are: "Where did David live as a child?" and "In the Bible, what book did Paul first write?"

Students have many, many experiences. Their experiences come, in a large part, from parents and community; therefore, Sunday school literature should describe some of the experiences involving parents. Usually the home situations lead students to experiences within the community. Many students can relate to situations that appear similar to situations that they have experienced. For example, what most children do at home could be done in the community. Therefore, a good curriculum should recognize the community. The literature will then interpret facts of present day society, describing what kind of society we live in. It will define Christian goals for society. Then it will present practical ways to face community problems.

Christian education is important for the African American community. The student learns from his or her community experiences. The literature should then reflect the African American experience, speak relevantly to the African American experience, and acknowledge one's social setting. A growth mode is needed for the African American child, youth, and adult. In other words, can the ghetto child, youth, or adult learn anything from the lesson? Symbols from the African American experience are very much needed in the literature. Imagery also communicates ideas and concepts to the various age levels; however, the degree of difficulty must be kept in mind. Some students have not been exposed to certain language or speech patterns; therefore, the teacher's awareness of students' communications and understandings of the language is vital. Why not have the African American student glance at Sunday school literature and read about the African American male, female, family, church, and preacher? Lessons should create a family setting. The African American student needs to envision his own family in the lesson.

If the African American child cannot see something that relates to what is happening in his or her life, like his or her own family, then the child might feel lost. Everybody wants to read about churches, families, or preachers who are examples for good leadership. This need causes the African American student to search for cultural roots and heritage.

The teacher can retrieve much African American published literature, when carefully searched. Urban Ministries in Chicago, and David C. Cook Publishing Company, Sunday School Publishing Board, National Baptist Publishing Board, and many other denominations provide literature from a partial African American perspective. I am not endorsing a particular literature, because all literature contains strengths and weaknesses.

According to Dr. Cain Felder, Benjamin Mays' findings remind us that: "There are instances in which Bible usage in many Black African American Churches had not attained the level of scriptural reinterpretation and pedagogy seen in first and second-century instructional materials" (*Troubling Biblical Waters* 87-88). Do not adapt literature that may not be appropriate for a certain group.

Again, I emphasize the need for the presence of African heritage in Sunday school literature. Walter McCray states that: "More and more people are becoming aware of the presence of Black people in Biblical history…Namely, that a significant number of Black, that is African, people are noted in the Scripture" (McCray ix).

Grant Shockley suggests that there are certain guidelines that one should consider when shaping Christian education to the Black experience:

1. A theoretical and operational education model that is conceptualized as an "empowering process for a powerless" minority. This model turns upside down most education models which seek to introduce the powerless into the ways of the powerful.

2. A cognitive model of learning that maximizes the biblical, historical, and theological sources and images of the Christian faith as authentically "for others" and pro-Black, without being anti-white.

3. A model of learning that is "holistic," i.e., it emphasizes the organic or "whole" nature of existence rather than the compartmentalization of life. It thus insures and guarantees a wide frame of reference for the inclusion of differences and uniqueness. In other words, pluralism lies at the heart of this alternative approach to Christian education.

4. A model of socialization that permits free interaction of ideas, concepts, customs, and heritages to intermingle without attending prejudices, with the result that all are enhanced. A new pattern of socialization is required — one that does not culminate in the assimilation of a minority people into the majority, but one that assumes that both majority and minority have cultural values, attitudes, and practices that are good and nurture us all into faithful Christians.

5. A model of leadership through which parents, teachers, pastors, and other church leaders can see and be influenced by what Carl Rogers calls the development of "fully functioning persons capable of impacting society." In other words, Black churchmen and women have to find a "comfortable group," which functions something like the former Black Central Jurisdiction of the Methodist Church in raising up leaders for the whole church. Until that time comes when leaders are chosen without any attention to color, there will need to be an opportunity for color-disadvantaged persons to assume leadership roles of significance. (16)

The objective in curriculum and in teaching from the African American experience may be seen from a contextual perspective. One can facilitate the learning of African American persons in a way that African Americans will realize "the God of the oppressed" and of "God's self-disclosure in the redemptive and empowering love of Jesus Christ, the liberator;" knowing themselves and the meaning of human situations and ways to "respond in love and faith through their Black Christian experience, personally and socially" (Shockley 17).

### CRITERION 6: DOES THE ARTWORK PROVIDE ENRICHMENT FOR AFRICAN AMERICAN STUDENTS?

In evaluating curriculum in the African American Church, viewing artwork may be helpful. The artwork is very important to the African American child. Artwork should be given special attention during the evaluation of children's literature. The evaluator might consider the following questions about the artwork: Does it depict persons of only the white race? Bible story-pictures should accurately depict dark-skinned people as well as Anglo-Saxon or other races. Are the buildings, and churches, all of one kind? Are the settings all uniform? The artwork could be one-sided since the aim is to appeal to one group of people. For example, if a Chinese person is portrayed, a Black child may not understand the real message. The African American child could possibly think that the message is only for the child portrayed. The artwork of buildings plays an important role for African Americans. The African American child wants to see buildings similar to the building he or she lives in. For example, the African American child who lives in the ghetto may not identify with a building where upper-class people live. Artwork might include buildings for the rich, middle-class, and poor.

### CRITERION 7: DOES THE ACTIVITY PACKET PROVIDE A LEARNING EXPERIENCE?

A good evaluator considers the activity packets. An activity packet is that set of materials that provide an activity, a self-expression, a game, or what I call an opportunity to get away from the book, yet continue learning the lesson. Many activity packets have maps, records, tapes, songs, charts, games, or other items for enrichment that provide opportunities for students.

The organization and purpose of curriculum should be kept in mind when selecting Sunday school literature:

> Those responsible for choosing the curriculum for a particular church should study the entire organization and purpose of each curriculum, and then make the decision as to which of the planned curricula best fits the local situation and comes closest to the ideal for the particular school in mind. (Byrne 126)

It is wise for the organization to have consultants to aid in selecting literature. The Joint Educational Development Approach states:

> A local congregation should have a curriculum planning and evaluation committee. The committee should attempt to keep the demands of the gospel in touch with the people's needs and their social situations, both locally and worldwide. (Miller, Donald 309)

One should look at least three different curricula before selecting Sunday school literature. If the denomination has selected the literature, supplementary literature should be evaluated for content and to maintain the denominational doctrine. Evaluating Sunday school literature can be time-consuming; however, the literature should not be selected at first sight.

## Conclusion

Who selects Sunday school literature? Most churches have constitutional requirements about who selects or approves Sunday school literature. The superintendent and the Christian Education Director are usually the persons who select Sunday school literature.

The first place to find out what is available is, of course, your denominational board. Most denominational boards have recommendations. If they do not recommend literature for your church, you should consider using literature that is appropriate for your students. In other words, if you have a mixed congregation (more than one ethnic group of persons), then one should consider a literature that will meet the needs of all. For example, the African American Church may consider using Sunday school literature from Urban Ministry, or Echoes Literature from David C. Cook Publishing Companies; or one may want to modify any present literature, if permission is granted by the denomination or publisher.

Selecting Sunday school literature can be challenging. It could lead a Sunday school to better attendance, and students could become more motivated. Selecting Sunday school literature should be done with much care and concern. The process for selecting Sunday school literature could include some of the processes I have mentioned in this chapter. I suggest that one consider the following: The person in charge of curriculum should select any literature that he or she thinks would meet the needs of their students. Select a team (teachers and leaders of the Sunday school) to evaluate the literature, keeping in mind the steps for evaluating Sunday school literature. Assign each set of material to a team for evaluation. There should be several groups or pairs evaluating the same literature. After this step is completed, share your findings, and go to the next set of literature that might be appealing.

If one does not desire to use Sunday school literature that is already on the market, one might consider writing Sunday school literature to meet specific needs. A curriculum writer would be helpful in assisting anyone writing curriculum.

# Evaluating the Sunday School Literature

*Michael Anthony Johnson*

# Chapter 4

# Developing Lesson Plans in the African American Sunday School

In order to develop lesson plans for the African American Church, I suggest that the teacher should carefully pray and plan for the class lessons. Anne Wimberly states: "We dare not envision Christian education processes without giving serious thought to the quality of settings in which the processes are to occur" (Wimberly 33). One should keep in mind, as I have stated, the institution for whom one is planning: the African American Church. The setting deserves the very best in education. This means that one should focus on content that the African student might find interesting, can identify with, and of course, will spiritually shape his or her life. Once the content or literature has been approved, one should proceed to develop the lesson plan. Much Sunday school literature includes a step-by-step process for teaching. The teacher should keep in mind that some literature does not clearly state goals or objectives in terms that students can understand. If this is the case, it is important for the teacher to know how to modify what he or she is using. In addition, there might be times when the teacher will have to pull out segments or rewrite the entire lesson plan to make it useful and appropriate. The teacher understands that no writer knows every people or area in which the literature will be used. In other words, the needs of your students may not be needs of other students. If your students already know about the Apostle Paul, why spend all of your time dealing with this apostle when other apostles should be discussed?

In this chapter, the focus will be on writing lesson plans. If one does not need every component, use whatever is helpful in writing your les-

# Developing Lesson Plans

son plans for the African American Sunday School. Specific attention will be given to steps for writing lesson plans. A clarification for each step is listed. In addition, a sample lesson plan will be provided.

> ### COMPONENTS FOR THE LESSON PLAN
> *Every lesson plan has a beginning, a middle, and an end.*
>
> I. Goal
> II. Main Idea
> III. Objective
> !V. The Lesson Design
> Step One: Beginning
> Step Two: Stating the Objective
> Step Three: Introducing the Content
> Step Four: Modeling the Content
> Step Five: Discovering the Content
> Step Six: Relating to the Content
> Step Seven: Concluding the Content
> Step Eight: Reinforcing the Content

## THE GOAL

As previously stated, the teacher should understand that his/her goal is to teach. Many times educators confuse goals with objectives. Let me briefly explain what a goal is.

According to Donald Griggs in the book *Teaching Teachers to Teach*, a goal is big enough to spend a lifetime pursing. The goal is beyond our reach. For example, we will never, yet some might try, achieve the goals of Christian living. Goals provide direction for learning and teaching. They are too general to aid in evaluating or planning activities (13)

**Writing Goals:** At the end of the session the student will be able to:

a. Realize...

b. Feel...

c. Know...

d. Understand...

Main Idea

The main idea gives the teacher a beginning for writing objectives. By definition, the main idea is the concept that the teacher wishes to present. Perhaps it is the value of kindness, or expressing love in relationships. It is a larger concept than just learning Bible verses.

An example of a main idea is:

African Americans are called by God to build great buildings. Solomon was called to build a temple.

Objectives

There are two kinds of objectives: behavioral and instructional. The behavioral objective can be measured and describes student performance. The instructional objective describes what content will be taught. For example, a behavioral objective might read: *Students will* be able to *list* the books of the Bible. The instructional objective might read: The student should complete the assigned homework. To include both objectives, one might state: The student will complete the homework by writing the names of the books of the Bible in alphabetical order (Briggs 16-20). All objectives are specific. They are written in terms of what should be accomplished. Objectives should be reasons for learning.

**EXAMPLES OF WORDING FOR OBJECTIVES:**
A. Demonstrate
B. List
C. State
D. Identify
E. Describe
F. Summarize
G. Show
H. Name
I. Explain

All of the words in the above table demonstrate something that can be seen. The teacher may state the condition, time, materials, and resources for each.

# Developing Lesson Plans

To test your objectives, ask yourself these questions: Does the objective describe what the student will be doing when he or she is demonstrating that he or she has reached the objective? Does the objective describe the important conditions under which the student will be expected to demonstrate his or her learning? Does the objective indicate how the student will be evaluated? Does it, at least, describe the lower limits of acceptable performance? Does the objective identify the specific content?

## THE LESSON DESIGN

The lesson design for a class session of approximately 45 to 60 minutes long should follow a specific plan.

---

**LESSON PLAN DESIGN**

1. Beginning
2. Stating the objective
3. Introducing the content
4. Modeling the content
5. Discovering the content
6. Relating to the content (Black experience)
7. Concluding the Content
8. Reinforcing the Content

---

### STEP ONE — BEGINNING

**Clarification:** The beginning of the session is very crucial for the class. The class should open with prayer. Prayer is very important for any opening. The teacher may pray or call on a volunteer student. Never force anyone to pray or embarrass a student. The way one starts off could well mean how one will end up. The opening could turn a student off or on. Usually if the teacher's opening remarks are interesting, the flow of the lesson plan will go well. The teacher may ask students to recall what happened in last week's lesson, or what happened in the community the past week.

Time frame: Three minutes.

## A Manual for Teacher-Training

STEP TWO — STATE THE OBJECTIVE IN STUDENT TERMS

**Clarification:** The teacher opens the class session by first giving the objective for the day. It does not have to be stated in the terms written, but in a way students may understand it. The teacher is stating the reason for learning and why.

Time frame: Approximately one minute.

STEP THREE — INTRODUCING THE CONTENT

**Clarification:** The teacher will present the subject by writing on the board, using an overhead projector, or by speaking to the class about concepts that will be learned in the lesson. The text should be given at this point.

Time frame: Approximately ten minutes.

STEP FOUR — MODELING THE CONTENT

**Clarification:** Modeling is very helpful. By modeling, use something eye-catching, or tell a story, present a skit that will introduce the lesson, invite a guest speaker, listen to excerpts from a sermon, or show a video, to name a few. In modeling, the teacher is going to show students a sample of what is needed. For example, if the teacher is teaching about a Black or African Jesus, the teacher might hold up a picture of a Black or African Jesus. If one is teaching about a country, continent, or certain area, a map should be used to actually show students the area. This is a good time for the teacher to introduce positive Black role models.

Time frame: Approximately three minutes.

STEP FIVE — DISCOVERING THE LESSON CONTENT

**Clarification:** The subject to be studied will be discussed in detail. The content of the lesson plan will be given at this point. Students may work in a group, or the teacher may lecture. Students may also work in learning centers, listen to recorded tapes on the subject, or research the Bible. Students might present projects to explain the lesson.

Time frame: Approximately 15 minutes

STEP SIX — RELATING TO THE CONTENT: THE BLACK EXPERIENCE

**Clarification:** The teacher gives the student an opportunity to respond in creative ways. The African American student may respond from

# Developing Lesson Plans

his or her own experience. The teacher should encourage this kind of response. The student may draw, dance, perform a skit, write poems or other expressions, make a collage, or do a variety of presentations at this point.

Time frame: Approximately eight minutes or longer

**STEP SEVEN — CONCLUDING THE CONTENT & UNDERSTANDING**

**Clarification:** Concluding is really the time to share what has been done. It is time to wrap-up or conclude the overall objective. This section is very important. The teacher should summarize or ask students to summarize points. The teacher may give a test or quiz, hand out worksheets, have the students show and tell, play a game with the students, or monitor as students play. By all means the teacher should encourage students to do some type of assignment for the next class, if no more than reading a Scripture. This assignment should not be long and does not have to be written. Keep in mind that there might be other classes, or jobs involved. The teacher or volunteer student should close with prayer.

Time frame: Approximately 5 to 15 minutes

**STEP EIGHT — REINFORCING THE CONTENT/GUIDED PRACTICE**

**Clarification:** The teacher assists the student with an assignment. Individual attention to every student could take too much time within the average time frame of an average class. Guided practice is also homework. The teacher should decide whether or not homework is beneficial, and if so, when will the teacher check it?

Remember that the lesson plan is designed to help guide the teacher through the lesson. There is always room for improvisation and improvement. The first thing to do is to decide what topic or subject one wants to deal with in the session; then the next step is prayer. Many times when the teacher's thoughts are fuzzy, prayer is needed to clarify the subject. In considering subjects for the African American student, one could write lesson plans from the following ideas.

> ### General Subjects for Lesson Plans, by Rev. Ronnie A. Clark
> *(Actual plans should be more specific)*
>
> 1. The family of Jesus, (John 7: 1-5) highlighting the African American family.
> 2. Family ancestors and family trees. (Gen. 10: 6-20, Numbers 26: 28-37)
> 3. Black ancestry of Jesus. (Matthew 1:1-16 ; Luke 3:23-38)
> 4. Shem and his descendants.
> 5. Japheth and his descendants. (Genesis 10: 2-5)
> 6. Glancing at Ethiopia.
> 7. The Cushites.
> 8. The families of the Canaanites. (Genesis 10:18b-19)
> 9. The sons and descendants of Ham.
> 10. The father of African peoples — Ham.
>
> *NOTE:* Any of the above could be used for a series of lessons.

## Illustrative Verbs for Stating Objectives

There are many verbs that I have used in my various teaching experiences. Some are: analyze, apply, compare, contrast, comprehend, complete, compute, demonstrate, distinguish, explain, interpret, listen, outline, perform, recite, speak, state, summarize, think, translate, and understand.

## A Sample Lesson Plan, By Janice Oliver

**Main Idea:** Hagar's ethnicity correlates with the modern African American conflict of racism. God makes a covenant with Abraham which ironically involves Abraham's servant, Hagar.

**Objective:** The student should be able to:

1. explain who Hagar and Abraham are in the Old Testament.
2. describe the covenant made between God and Abraham.

## Developing Lesson Plans

3. define the terms: conceived, barren, Hebrews, Egyptians, and harlot.

4. describe why Hagar was jealous of Sarah.

**Beginning:** The teacher reads a brief background statement about Africa and Egypt, describing the areas where Sarah and Hagar were from. Have the students read aloud Genesis 16: 1-16. Divide students into groups of three's. Each group will discuss the reading. Students will choose a leader from each group to lead discussion.

**Stating the Objective:** *see* "Objectives" above.

**Introducing the Content:** The teacher writes the definitions of the words: barren, conceived, harlot, Egyptians, and Hebrews on the chalkboard. The teacher goes over each word. The students will lead a discussion on what it is like being a different nationality/ethnic group, with reference to Hagar — an Egyptian living among Hebrews. Have students correlate those feelings with feelings of African Americans living in a society that is dominated by non-African Americans.

Resources: *Bible Dictionary*

**Modeling the Content:** The teacher will use a map to show the areas of Africa and Egypt, emphasizing where Hagar and Sarah came from.

Resources: *Bible Encyclopedia,* map, and a Bible for opening and modeling.

**Discovering the Content:** Who was Hagar? Who was Abraham? Who was Sarah? Why was Hagar jealous of Sarah?

Resources: *Bible Dictionary,* Bible, *Bible Encyclopedia*

**Relating to the Content:** Students will role-play Abraham, Sarah, and Hagar.

**Concluding the Content:** Students will write a brief paragraph explaining the values of the Hagar story.

Resources: paper, pens, pencils

**Reinforcing the Content:** Students will be given a list of questions to complete at home. Answers will come from Genesis 16: 1-16.

## Evaluation of Teacher Lesson Plans

To evaluate lesson plans, ask the following questions:

1. Do the main ideas and objectives seem appropriate for the age group? Older students may need the entire story taught, while younger students need only parts of the story taught.

2. Do the main ideas and objectives directly connect? If the story about Hebrews being slaves in Egypt is discussed as the main idea, the objective should relate to the subject or theme. A discussion about contemporary slavery is not appropriate because Hebrews might have had a different experience of slavery.

3. Did the teacher ask questions during the session? Students need to be encouraged to think and apply subjects to daily living.

4. Are examples of the African American life-style included? Students need to vision themselves.

5. Does the lesson include an activity? The lesson should include a variety of ways for students to learn.

6. Does the room arrangement facilitate the achievement of the objective? How tables, chairs, visuals, and/or bulletin and chalk boards are going to be arranged should be noted.

7. Are students motivated?

(Revised from the Griggs model 44-46)

# Developing Lesson Plans

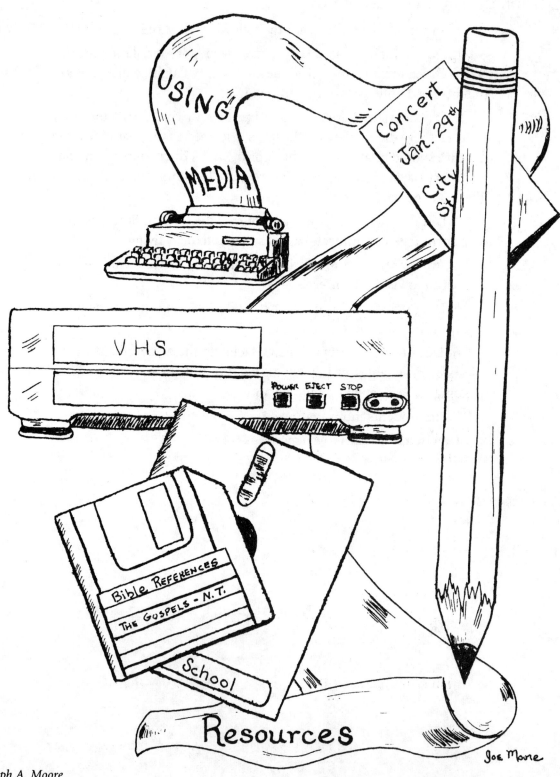

*Rev. Joseph A. Moore*

# Using Media Resources

One's African American Church should own some media equipment or at least be able to borrow it. In some cases, Sunday school teachers and superintendents use their creative resources when Sunday school supplies cannot be purchased. It is wise for the African American Church to consider investing in its own equipment. Many churches do not have media funds. It seems that some churches place little emphasis upon spending money for Sunday schools because they do not see the value for purchasing the materials. I suggest that every church own the following:

1. A television (preferably a wide-screen, if possible)
2. A video recorder
3. An overhead projector
4. Some type of chalkboard or other writing board
5. A tape recorder

A television can be used for showing Christian movies to all age groups. After the movie, the class may discuss the movie.

The video recorder will enable one to play videos and to record Christian films. Include videos from the Afrocentric experience.

The overhead projector may be used for teacher prepared materials; student reports; student creativity, such as illustrating a story; map study, such as learning about the land where Jesus lived; opaque collages such as toothpicks, popsickle sticks, strings, and rubber bands to create im-

## Using Media Resources

ages; and photos from books or magazines, to mention a few. Points may be made on the chalkboard. Every classroom should have some type of board.

The tape recorder may be used for many purposes. The recorder may be used for children to listen to prerecorded Scripture or for them to record their own reading of Scripture, for group activities, or to play other religious recordings. In addition, one could own or rent filmstrip projectors, 16mm projectors, slide projectors, and so on.

The basic criteria for purchasing equipment are:

1. Will the resource enhance the education of students in the African American Church?

2. Are students more motivated to learn about God at work in the African American Church?

3. Is the resource appropriate for the age group?

4. Does the resource allow an introduction to a subject by presenting basic information clearly and objectively?

### About Videos, Movies, & Slides

It is very important to preview videos and movies prior to showing them, Careful attention should be given to characters, Christian aims, content/language, and illustrations. A video or movie should not be shown because the teacher did not prepare for the day's lesson.

# Chapter 6

# Suggested Workshops for the African American Church

Following are some ideas for workshops aimed at the African American Sunday School teachers.

1. Who Are Your Pupils?
2. Ways of Understanding African American Children.
3. How to Aim Your Activities at Teaching Faith.
4. The Origin of the African American Sunday School.
5. Ways to Motivate the African American Student.
6. The Unique Teacher for the African American Sunday School.
7. Bridging the Gap of Yesterday and Today.
8. Social Concerns Play a Big Role in the African American Sunday School.
9. Teachings from African Biblical Roots.
10. The Role of the Pastor in Christian Education.
11. Writing Sunday School Literature for the African American Church.
12. Methods for Teaching in the Classroom.

**Suggested Workshops**

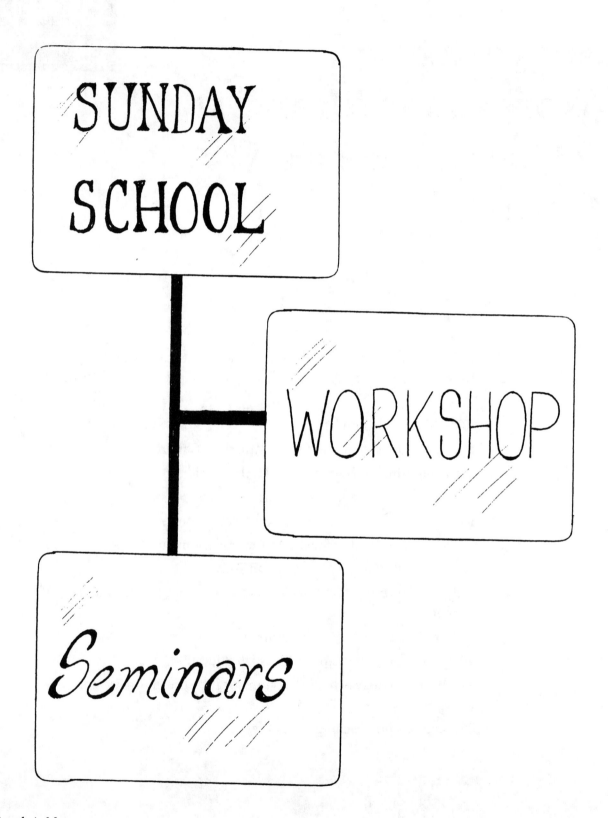

*Rev. Joseph A. Moore*

# Chapter 7

# Future Suggestions for Christian Education in the African American Church

This manual will only act as one seed for the African American Church Educational Program. I would like to present the following suggestions for the African American Church:

1. The pastor should become more active in Christian education.
2. Budget considerations for Christian education should be rethought and made a priority.
3. African American Churches need to consider pooling resources.
4. Parents need to show more concern for Christian education.
5. Leaders need to distinguish "fun" activities from "learning activities."
6. The African American Church should teach the entire community, not only church members.
7. Educators need to develop methods to "draw" students rather than "run" students from the church.
8. Consider developing Sunday school lessons that include Afrocentric history and African American experiences.
9. Churches should consider employing a "trained" Christian education director, or hiring a director who is willing to receive training.

The pastor is the lock to the Christian educational program. God has provided the key; but, often, the pastor removes the lock and intruders "break in" or "walk in," destroying the Christian Educational Pro-

## Future Suggestions

gram. The pastor's first step in promoting Christian education is providing a "lock." In other words, the pastor needs to guard the Christian education program. Whatever happens or does not happen reflects upon his or her leadership. This is why the pastor needs to constantly seek education or upgrade skills for a modern society. If the pastor shows no or little interest in his/her own education, parishioners might become less interested in Christian education. A pastor should always remember to practice what is preached. If Christian education is recommended, never forget to seek training or update skills for oneself. If the pastor has not sought theological training of some sort, seeking some type of religious education, if no more than discussing new ways to upgrade one's program (according to one's ability). What if the Holy Spirit wants to speak through someone other than you?

The church budget should include Christian education as a major priority. Church leaders need to understand that money is needed to "train." Disciples become disciples through training. Too many leaders have neglected preparation for responsibilities, including many pastors who lead congregations, simply because of the lack of funds and/or little faith.

The pooling of resources means churches making a joint effort to promote spiritual growth. This means educating parishioners to understand why the church needs to develop a center for the community, county, or city, as their African American Church Educational Resource Center. It might mean more than one or two churches coming together for a cooperative effort. This means that denominational values should not hinder the cooperative action for learning. The pooling of resources does not necessitate modifying denominational principals or doctrines, but provides an opportunity to look at supplementary materials for teacher-education, and allows African Americans to encourage the church to be the most effective institution in the community. The church could and should own grocery stores, clothing stores, and other necessary stores for African American Christians to be fed spiritually *and* physically. Pastors need to encourage parishioners to view the church as meeting human needs, both spiritually and physically.

Parents have a responsibility in promoting Christian education. This means that the parent(s) should first begin at home. The parent(s) need to take "charge" of children 18 and under. If the parent(s) goes to church, then the child or children should be instructed, not asked, to attend church, including Sunday school and Bible school. I challenge parents to be more aware of the need for student attendance, and organize a strategy to reach the unreached, beginning first at home.

So often church leaders do not distinguish "fun" activities from "creative activities." Leaders who suggest field trips simply out of tradition or because field trips are thought of as somewhere for children to go, might not be carefully planning learning activities for spiritual insights. It is my hope that church leaders give more attention to the programs offered *in* the church.

In all planning, the church should have a weekly worship bulletin and an educational flow chart that include educational offerings for the entire community. The African American Church is no longer effective to simply serve those in the pews. There are many people sitting on the church "steps," simply because too many churches cater only to members.

Educators can "draw" students *to* the church or "run" them *from* the church. Educators need to rethink methods for teaching. Many African American Sunday Schools still use the archaic view of having students read and explain Bible verses as the total learning experience in the Sunday school. I encourage educators to consider other teaching methods. How can students explain Bible verses read in Sunday school books if students have not been taught what the verses mean?

Churches that instruct African American students need to encourage leaders, educators, and curricula writers to carefully research Afrocentric ideas prior to developing an Afrocentric curriculum. Some authors who write about Afrocentric views may not be familiar with the "whole" African culture. Then, too, some authors write from the Eurocentric view. How can the curricula writer determine "good" from "bad" scholarship? I suggest that one know the author's background: education and experience for writing about the subject, consider research skills and other scholarly publications.

Christian Afrocentric curricula would first include Biblical content. Then, include history.

Lastly, churches should consider employing a full-time Christian education director. There is still a lack of Christian educators with a theological or educational degree in Christian education. A full-time director could fill many gaps in Christian education. For example, The offering of daytime classes could be the key for people who cannot attend nighttime Bible classes. Also, the Christian education director could assess

# Future Suggestions

educational needs and develop strategies to meet those needs will be most valuable.

The Christian education director should be trained. If one does not have a degree, seeking some education will be helpful. Attending workshops is only one way to train Christian leaders. Keep in mind workshop leaders who have been educated in Christian education. Experienced leaders may not be educated leaders. Remember, if the church invests "cheap" dollars for training workshops, "cheap" results will follow.

*Professor Alexis Joyner*

# Works Cited

**INTRODUCTION**

Griggs, Donald. *Teaching Teachers To Teach.* Nashville: Abingdon Press, 1983.

**CHAPTER 1**

Asante, MoleFi. *The Afrocentric Idea.* Philadelphia: Temple University Press, 1987.

Chism, Keith Allan. *Developing a Model for Teacher Training within the Black Church Context.* D. Min. published dissertation, United Theological Seminary, 1990.

Frazier, Edward Franklin. *The Negro Church in America.* New York: Schocken Books, 1974.

Goodwin, Bennie E. *Steps to Dynamic Teaching.* Atlanta: Goodpatrick Publishers, 1980.

Griggs, Donald L. *Teaching Teachers to Teach.* Nashville: Abingdon Press, 1983.

Williams, Willard A. *Educational Ministries With Blacks.* Nashville: The Board of Discipleship of the United Methodist Church, 1974.

**CHAPTER 3**

Byrne, H. W. *Improving Church Education.* Birmingham: Religious Education Press, 1979.

Crockett, Joseph. *Teaching Scripture from the African American Perspective.* Nashville: Disciples Resources, 1994.

Cully, Iris. *Planning and Selecting Curriculum for Christian Education.* Valley Forge: Judson Press, 1983.

Doll, Ronald C. "Twenty Questions About Sunday-School Materials." *Christianity Today,* March, 1972.

Felder, Cain, Hope. *Stony the Road We Trod—African American Biblical Interpretation.* Minneapolis: Fortress Press, 1991.

# Works Cited

---------*Troubling Biblical Waters—Race, Class, and Family.* Mary Knoll: Oris Books, 1989.

Frazier, Edward Franklin. *The Negro Church in America.* New York: Schocken Books, 1963.

*From Guide To Curriculum Choice.* Elgin: Brethren Press, 1981.

Goodwin, Bennie II. *Effective Teaching Series, Steps to Dynamic Teaching.* Atlanta: GoodPatrick Publishers, 1980.

----------------. *The Effective Leader-A Basic Guide to Christian Leadership.* Atlanta: GoodPatrick Publishers, 1989.

Griggs, Donald. *Teaching Teachers to Teach.* Nashville: Abingdon Press, 1983.

Hilliard, Asa G, et al. *Infusion of African and African American Content in the School Curriculum.* (Proceedings of the First National Conference, October , 1989) Morristown: Aaron Press, 1990.

Joint Educational Manual- *Perspectives in Church Education-*"Role of Function of Resources."

Leavitt, Guy P. *Superintend with Success.* Cincinnati: Standard Publishing Company, 1989 .

Love, Mary A. "Musings on Sunday School in the Black Community." *Renewing the Sunday School and the CCD.* Edited by Dewitte Campbell Wyckoff. Birmingham: Religious Education Press, 1986.

McCray, Walter. *The BLACK Presence in the BIBLE.* Chicago: Black Light Fellowship, 1990.

Miller, Donald E. *Story and Context—An Introduction to Christian Education.* Nashville: Abingdon Press, 1987.

Miller, Randolph. "Theology in Background." *Religious Education and Theology.* Edited Norma H. Thompson. Birmingham, Alabama: Religious Education Press, 1982.

Olivia Stokes. "Black Theology: A Challenge to Religious Education." *Religious Education and Theology.* Editor Norma H. Thompson. Birmingham: Religious Education Press, 1982.

Poindexter, Marion."Curriculum Class Notes," 1986 Drew University.

*Report developed during Krisheim II Conference on Education Resources for Black Churches,* September 3, 1970, Sponsored by the Black Christian Education Administrative and Co-ordinating Committee.

Sandidge, Oneal C. *Selecting Sunday School Literature in the Black Church.* D. Min. published dissertation, Drew University, 1992.

Shockley, Grant S. *Christian Education Journey of Black Americans— Past, Present, Future.* Nashville: Discipleship Resources, 1985.

Williams, Williard A. *Educational Ministries With Blacks.* Nashville: The Board of Discipleship of the United Methodist Church, 1974),16-24. The entire section on rehumanization is studied from this book.

Wyckoff Campbell DeWitte, Ed. *How to Evaluate Your Christian Education Program.* Philadelphia: The Westminster Press, 1962.

## CHAPTER 4

Abatso, Yvonne and George Abatso. *How to Equip the African American Family—Issues and Guidelines for Building Strong Families.* Chicago: Urban Ministries, Inc., 1991.

Briggs, Leslie. *Handbook of Procedures For The Design of Instruction.* Florida: American Institutes for Research, 1970.

Griggs, Donald L. *Teaching Teachers to Teach.* Nashville: Abingdon Press, 1983.

Hunter, Madelin. *Improved Instruction.* El-Sungundo, California: Tip Publication, 1976.

McCray, Walter Arthur. *The BLACK Presence in the BIBLE.* Chicago: Black Light Fellowship, 1990.

Wimberly, Anne. *Soul Stories: African American Christian Education.* Nashville: Abingdon, 1994.

## CHAPTER 5

Fowler, Floyd J. *Research Methods.* Beverly Hills: Sage Publications, 1984.

Griggs, Donald L. *Teaching Teachers to Teach.* Nashville: Abingdon Press, 1974.

## FOR COMMENTS/WORKSHOPS/PREACHING, CONTACT:

AGENT FOR REV. DR. ONEAL SANDIDGE
P.O. Box 56971
Atlanta, GA 30343

## About the Author

Dr. Oneal Cleaven Sandidge is a licensed and ordained forty year-old preacher who received ministerial direction under the direction of Rev. George Bolden, Jr. He was reared in Amherst County, Virginia. He is member of The Timothy Baptist Church in Amherst County, Virginia.

Oneal holds the following earned degrees: Doctor of Ministry from Drew University, Madison, New Jersey; Master of Religion and American Education from Columbia University, New York, New York: Master of Religious Education from Howard University, Washington, D.C,; Bachelor of Arts in Religious and Elementary Education from Lynchburg College, Lynchburg, Virginia. He is a graduate of Amherst High School, Amherst, Virginia. He has done further study at University of Virginia, Virginia Union School of Theology. In 1992 Oneal was selected a Merrill's Fellow at Harvard University, Cambridge, Massachusetts. In 1993, he was selected Fellow for the Southside Virginia Writing Project, Virginia State University and took graduate writing classes.

Oneal has taught middle school English and History, and all upper elementary subjects for eight years, History of the Black Church at Piedmont Virginia Community College, and Christian Education and other subjects at Virginia Seminary and College. He has taught for National Baptist, U.S. Christian Education Convention. He was guest lecturer for Hampton Minister's Conference in the Christian education division, 1993. He has written various articles including: *The Howard University Journal* "The Uniqueness of Black Preaching," and a number of articles in Christian education. He has written for *Leadership Magazine,* United Methodist Church Headquarters, Nashville, Tennessee. He has served churches in Virginia for many years. He is a member of many clubs and professional organization, including Kappa Delta Pi Honor Society at Columbia University.

Presently, Dr. Sandidge is assistant professor of Christian education at Luther Rice College and Seminary and visiting professor at Beulah Heights Bible College, both in the Atlanta area.